Ian Duhig

The Blind Roadmaker

PICADOR

First published 2016 by Picador
an imprint of Pan Macmillan
20 New Wharf Road, London N1 9RR
Associated companies throughout the world
www.panmacmillan.com

ISBN 978-1-5098-0981-3

1 3 5 7 9 8 6 4 2

A CIP catalogue record for this book is available from the British Library.

Printed and bound by CPI Group (UK) Ltd, Croydon, CR0 4YY

Contents

The Blind Roadmaker

Half the Story

Franz Kafka, the story goes, encountered a little girl in the park where he walked regularly. She was crying. She'd lost her doll. Kafka helped the girl search for the doll but they couldn't find it. They arranged to meet there next day to look again for her doll, but still they could not find it. When they met for the third time, Kafka gave her a tiny letter that he told her he'd found nearby. She read, 'Don't be sad: I'm only travelling. I'll write I promise!' And every day that summer, when Kafka and the little girl met, he'd read a new letter to her describing places the doll visited, what it did there and who it met. The little girl was comforted. When the holiday was over and she had to go back to school, he gave her a doll that he said was the lost prodigal returned, and, if it seemed a little different from the doll of her memory, a note pinned to its scarf explained: 'My travels changed me.'

Or so ends this version of the story, popular with therapists, but in Dora Diamant's own account, our one first-hand source, there was no new doll, nor a message of change and growth; instead, Dora had described a final letter sent to the little girl detailing how the doll met its soul mate and had married him; how it would be too busy with its new family to write again, enjoining the little girl to seek similar fulfilment in her own life. Dora also noted how this affair had driven Kafka to distraction, who'd endured white nights, tortured by his own compassion, feverishly thinking up new adventures for his changeling doll made out of letters and lies and love; how this correspondence had been maintained in this fashion for a period of three weeks – as long as that holiday when Dora Diamant had first met Franz, a place with a name that I only half-recall now, Graal-something.

The Blue Queen of Ashtrayland

What the fuck's the Holy Grail?
— Molly in *Urban Grimshaw and the Shed Crew*

Her hair glows, burnished as the gold
that trims her Nike cardigan;
Ionian white her Fila trainers,
DKNY jeans and cap.

Her skin's as blue as old skimmed milk;
as blue the star on her left cheek —
a Borstal beauty spot, tattooed
with broken glass and laundry ink.

The downers downed, the brown all tooted,
the homegrown hydroponic skunk
all shotgunned, blown-back, jointed, bonged,
the Queen calls for her royal Swan.

Through snakebite piercings on her lips
the bitten red adaptor hissed
like Cleopatra's asp its gas.
Our Queen jerks upright, claps her hands.

With no round table, they hand round
White Lightning in two-litre flasks.
She necks a draught then kicks her minstrel:
Skeeter fills the block with song,

'Bring me my Dig of burning gold,
Bring me Viagra of desire!
Bring me my foil: O, clouds unfold!
Bring me my Milligrams of Fire!'

Her knights take off to rob a dealer.
Urban's passed out on his crate.
Peeling back a cardboard curtain,
their Queen looks down on her estate.

Blockbusters

He lives in Leeds, completely out of the literary world.
— John Freeman, ex-Editor *Granta*

Thrillers like The Da Vinci Code *are key indicators of contemporary ideological shifts.*
— Slavoj Žižek, *In Defence of Lost Causes*

For what might break the grip that held my pen
so fast I couldn't write another line
I quested through the shops of Lady Charity
in Urbs Leodiensis Mystica,
the Shed Crew's capital of Ashtrayland,
a town beyond the literary world
whose locals speak blank verse (says Harrison);
Back-to-Front Inside-Out Upside-Down Leeds,
according to the Nuttgens book I bagged –
along with others offering keys to open
secrets of iambic pentameter,
to them, a ball and chain, a waltz – or best,
in Žižek's windsock for the New World Order,
Gnostic code imprinted by five feet
that lead us to a grail Brown liquefies,
as Shakespeare sometimes turns this line himself
to deliquescent decasyllabics
like the blood of St Januarius.
Brown quotes from Philip's Gospel (where it suits)
to build on Rosslyn Chapel's premises
his castle perilously in the air

while staying blind to mysteries below,
such as why you'll see Rosslyn's masons carved
among the seven virtues Greed,
and then set Charity with deadly sins . . .
The world was made in error Philip wrote –
Savonarola, in *The Rule of Four*,
another blockbuster from Oxfam's shelves
that followed in the footprints of Dan Brown,
is made to quote 'the Gospel of St Paul' . . .
is this the fault of slipshod editing
or does it hint perhaps at secret truth?
What if 'Paul's Gospel' really did exist?
What if it was some long-lost Gnostic text
thrown on the Bonfire of the Vanities
but glimpsed once by our zealot's burning eyes
who then confided to the ancestors
of those that seemed just greedy novelists
a hidden road map to the Holy Grail
a blind man saw on his Damascus road?

My back-to-back looks on a blind man's road
that runs due north from here past Wilfrid's city,
Shandy Hall then on to Lindisfarne
whose monks St Wilfrid was once sent from Rome
to knock back into shape from toe to top,
their sinful tops being 'Simon Magus tonsures',
that Gnostic wizard and heresiarch
the dog denounces in St Peter's Acts,
where that saint brings smoked tuna back to life,
explains his crucifixion upside-down

and how God's Kingdom could be found on Earth:
Make right your left, back forwards, low your high,
a realm inverted on our retinas,
much like Creation in the Gnostic view –
then, in a flash, like Paul, I saw the light
through Peter's apophatic paradox
to Stevens' definition of a poem,
a mirror-image of Frost's melting ice,
the fiery self-consuming meteor
but one surviving as 'the stone from heaven',
Wolfram Von Eschenbach's holy grail –
and knowing this, my pen was free again
like that sword Arthur freed from its own block,
but mightier and greedy for the words
so close to silence they're worth more than gold.
My quest was ended: I began to write
this poem backwards, as Da Vinci might.

The Plagiarist's Song

He's Dante's thief, shifty between *Is*,
so many serpents shedding selves,
lying as that is how he goes to work

for *Plagiarus* also means 'seducer':
sticky fingers between your sheets,
stolen kisses, lip service as unpaid

as Hell or Dante's debt to Ibn 'Arabī
whose Sharia takes thieves' hands
but not their letters, their signatures,

not yours too truly, all too faithfully
getting under skin enough to pass,
or to make a pass as if from you.

He'll contraceive what you most love
for one-night stanzas in your mask.
You won't know you've got his clap.

Bert Lloyd

Inventing people like 'Tom Cook'
   as sources for a song
in versions Bert himself cooked up
   was ethically wrong,

but if once Reynardine flashed eyes
   and then for Bert flashed teeth,
still Reynardine would recognize
   his passion underneath.

Which line was written by Bert Lloyd
   the song won't care, of course,
nor we who plays the Mari Lwyd
   or who's the hobby horse.

When Burton savaged plagiarism,
   Sterne did so in turn
but using Burton's words verbatim –
   one reason we love Sterne.

'Down by the Salley Gardens'
   Yeats plagiarized Anon:
the very same Bert credited
   in blank masks he put on.

Ghost-writing for his unborn ghosts
    perfected Bert's own style;
his Lorca beats most other versions
    by a country mile.

A mark of Nature, we've been told's
    abhorrence of a void;
it's natural I sound like Bert,
    the multiphonic Lloyd.

The Ballad of Blind Jack Metcalf

on the unveiling of his statue in Knaresborough

Verse by the numbers, numbered years
   summing up the dead;
small fingers feeling headstone faces –
   how young Jack learnt to read.

A man, he read behind their words
   how men and women felt,
like faces, suits and numbers stamped
   on tavern cards he dealt.

Sharp dealer, traffic was Jack's gift,
   in fish and flesh he'd trade;
a soldier, smuggler, fiddler, guide –
   roadmaker, when that paid.

He'd spin his tales and webs of tar
   as dark as all he saw;
he was our Daedalus of roads,
   we're each his Minotaur –

Asterions, his starry ones,
   we travel by his lights
a hundred thousand miles each day,
   his thousand and one nights.

Still dark in bronze on Market Square,
  he hears the high road snarling
who heard them sing the Bonnie Prince –
  but traffic's still Jack's darling.

His waywiser beside his bench,
  around his metalled hat
his secret tale's picked out in braille
  and what it says is that . . .

The Balladeer's Lament

My forms will never warm these hares;
   not here nor there, they turn again
their free verse from my poem's course
   for mazes their own brains lay down.

They slip my words as easily
   as they their shapes and English gods
to please themselves, their world a breeze,
   still new their tricks. Too old this dog.

The Wold Is Everything That Is The Case

after Edwin Morgan

the wo ld is everything that is the case
the wo ld is   th is case
the wor d is everything that is the case
the wor d is every   case
the world is   a t e ase
the world is   at i t
the world is eve
the world is   he
the world s ing
the wo ld s ing
the wor d s ing
the   thing is e ase
the wo ld is everything
the wor d is everything
the wor d is everything that is the case
the wo ld is everything that is the case
the world is everything that is the case

[13]

Sternomancy

An Irish bull is always pregnant
– John Pentland Mahaffey

Completely misconstruing the word 'Sternomancy'
in Creech's version of the Third Book of Pantagruel,
I took to calculating chance via *Sortes Shandeanae*
sticking a knife between the pages of my 1783 Sterne
as if to find a name for dada in the French dictionary.

I first turned a warning: *Go not further into this thorny
and bewildered track, intricate are the steps! intricate
are the mazes of this labyrinth! intricate the troubles
the pursuit of this bewitching phantom KNOWLEDGE
will bring upon thee . . .* too late. I was already bewitched.

I used the knife again: *If I thought you were able to form
the least judgement or probable conjecture to yourself
of what is to come in the next page, – I would tear it
out of my book . . .* But I knew the myth of authorial intent.
On the third time of trying, I found a voice: *Speaking*

of my book as a machine . . . it reminded me of Calvino,
whose tarot was 'a narrative combinatorial machine'.
I knew I was on the right track, especially when I read
Though man is of all others the most curious vehicle,
hobbyhorse centaur. Rider, like the tarot deck's name.

Ridden too, interchanging their atoms as I interfaced
with Sterne. I read *as sure as I am I and you are you –*
and who are you? said he. Don't puzzle me; said I . . .
Now my flesh grains like calfskin binding; my speech
fills with dashes, ellipses, my lungs with ink like blood.

The calfskin grows into an Irish bull. I grow its head,
a minotaur in a labyrinth I built, stalked by this poem.
I feel its blade sliding down, along, between my ribs,
then rounding on my swollen stomach like a scalpel
rehearsing its lines before making the Caesarian cut.

The Marbled Page

For Aristotle, marble's motley
trapped gobs of first matter
from the moment of Creation
when Fortune mothered God.

Book-makers painted Her face
on gum-dragon, alum, ox-gall,
flea-seed and carrageen moss;
it moved on these new waters.

With such ink, a pen feathers;
a quill puns itself into a swan.
The twig in its beak-nib bursts
into marbled leaf, marbled tree.

Its bark is our word for book:
this being Sterne's machine,
he trusts a Deus ex machina
for providence of sentences.

His turn astern or go forth,
multiply like spiral galaxies
or live cells coming together
in the lens of a microscope.

His wild words whirl and whorl,
spinning from Fortune's wheel,
the author priest watches over
the reproduction of his design.

But the printing-shop is crowded.
For a moment, Sterne looks away.
The book-maker clears his throat
and gobs into the marbling trough.

Indirections

Askew from Skewsby, but not too far;
a few miles' digression from Shandy Hall
(though harder to find than Shangri-La)
they built a new Troy without any walls
or signposts, as if to thwart invasions;
remaining unmarked on motoring maps,
this smallest of all Britain's turf mazes
was never designed as a tourist trap,
but turns like a sonnet to trap Old Nick
as he can only move in a straight line,
the locals say, who might seem thick,
being shy of strangers and their designs –
but if in the end they choose to speak,
it sounds like Trojan, or Crooked Greek.

Shapeshifting Ghosts of Byland Abbey

In a note to his 'Twelve medieval ghost-stories', M.R. James explained that a monk of Byland Abbey had collected them locally, written them down then hid them in an unrelated manuscript. He noted this text's difficult handwriting, its 'refreshing' Latin, confusion, later moralising Christian editorial hand and resemblance more to Danish legends than anything native to these islands.

In one of the tales here, a man meets 'something like a horse' (one incarnation of the Gytrash, as a later commentator noted) which turns into 'a whirling heap of hay with light in the middle'. Changing into human form, it told him why it haunted that spot. When the man arranged absolution for this spirit with a priest, it was freed from its ghostly state and never seen there again.

In another story, a man is attacked at night by a large crow; sparks flew from its wings as if from a blacksmith's hammer, but when he drew out his sword and stabbed at the creature, 'it seemed more as if he was striking at a peat-stack'. Then it appeared as a dog with a chain about its neck; looking inside its jaws, the man could see deep into inside its belly, where a furnace was burning.

One ghost came as a bleating goat, subsequently turning into a huge man, 'horrible-looking, thin as one of the Dead Kings in a painting'. A different Byland spirit 'looked like a thorn-bush or a bonfire'; one appeared to be 'a bullock without a mouth, eyes or ears'. I have heard tell of another which 'looked at first a bull, became a cock and then became a bull again.

In a story not included in the Latin original of James' collection, from another oral source, a ghost came as a bull-headed man to a monk one night, who thought it a vision of St Luke, as he had been illuminating Luke's gospel at that time. *But when it spake*, he said, *I knew it was no vision of a saint*. This monk was later burnt for trafficking in a Gnostic heresy.

The Golden Calf

Like one of his pickled farm animals,
this loiner artist now divides himself:
on one side, a brainless gilded calf,
painting from spin, a diamanté skull.

The other half? A calf's head rots,
St Luke incarnated in a glass box,
as flocks of unconverted maggots
digest his gospel message. Watch:

one by one, they are born again:
the albs of maggots burst apart
to show off new black hair shirts;
as their stained-glass wings open,

one by one the saved souls rise
towards the electric blue skies
of the built-in insect-o-cutors.
Now that really created a buzz.

'Combat Gnosticism'

Campbell's term for war writing born
of a gnosis only being there can earn:
I witnessed it once from old soldiers
in a poetry workshop at Age Concern.

They'd lost that battle with the word,
believing too much better left unsaid
to the likes of me and not those pals
now threescore and ten years dead.

How many old soldiers does it take
to change a lightbulb? asked one.
You can't know if you weren't there!
They all fell about. Now they'd won.

Relaxed, they began letting it out
into grey shades of afternoon light,
into words they feared betrayed it.
And I learned why they were right.

The Year's Mind, Ripon

The graves shiver beside the Poorhouse
as midnight prayers to the God of Hosts
drift down to the obelisk in Market Place,
a Cleopatra's needle for bonelace ghosts.

Dead hand-loom weavers spin and reel
as sin-eaters flinch from witch-smellers;
the Risen of the North surround a Dean
who sold bells for wine to fill his cellars.

Still nursing his plastic two-litre bottle,
a squaddie suicide drips slowly past
with that Buckfast and tequila cocktail
the local police have nicknamed *Killfast*.

The Clock warns '*Except ye Lord keep
ye Cittie ye Wakeman waketh in vain*';
vain the fool waking those not asleep.
The Skell gathers itself to drown again.

Canto

If *canto*'s rooted in the Latin word for song,
    it harmonizes here with English 'cant',
so often wriggling on Lord Byron's prong
    and target of that *Tristram Shandy* rant
where he deems critics guiltiest of this wrong –
    but I am led already to descant,
a wandering fault that I, like Byron, caught from Sterne.
Now to our tale directly will we turn

with deejay DJ falling in the war . . .
    well, for a woman soldier home on leave.
Being short of time, she truly knew the score
    and played love games that you would not believe –
his shuttlecock served by her battledore . . .
    to cut this Tristramsquely short, he'd grieve
when duty called on whom he had a crush
    (for all his hard-ons, DJ's soul was mush).

Camilla was the name in DJ's heart,
    Camilla, Virgil's Volscian amazon,
Camilla, who felled DJ with love's dart,
    who was our Charlie's queen, and then was gone –
who for him (he thought) didn't give a fart,
    who'd loved and left him (as once he'd've done)
at exactly when she told him she would go
to fight whom politicians made her foe.

The myth that men made Brits a warrior race
    not Boudicca nor Thatcher could destroy.
Romanticizing writers liked to trace
    this nation's founding to the Fall of Troy,
when Brutus fled here, claimed and named this place
    in tales possessing that *je ne sais quoi*
our French conquering warriors liked to hear,
to make up for our weather, food and beer.

Apollo shipped with Brutus to this shore,
    the god of verse who orders me about,
who took this job for me (which is a bore),
    demanding, like a Cossack with a knout,
I get his show back on the road once more
    so off we go (before he starts to shout
the odds) to remake an old classic,
which I must do because I am borassic.

The way to a man's heart, a woman knows,
    runs straighter than the M1 through his penis –
this only could sound cynical to those
    who've looked at us but haven't really seen us;
straight or gay, we're pricks on true love's rose –
    junk science makes out women come from Venus
while most men aren't remote from *Life on Mars*:
such amatoria's now all my ars.

'What kind of poet speaks such treachery?
    The lad's a cad or mad or sad or bad!
Throughout this art's star-studded history,
    love's all some of its greatest poets had
to write our nation's greatest poetry,
    unlike this doggerel Gonadiad
whose author's even thicker than he looks
and needs to buy himself some proper books!'

Is *any* romance not 'self-love à deux'?
    No selfish gene's imperative,
but to that starry-eyed romantic, 'the
    best reason human beings have to live'?
I ask, but stricken DJ just grunts 'Huh?'
    To care requires a toss he doesn't give,
and every answer's anyway debatable –
which proves to him, at least, that love's inflatable.

'There's something in a huge balloon . . .' you'll note
    this empty joke's from Wordsworth's 'Peter Bell'
for DJ doomed on emptiness to dote,
    who was now of his old self just a shell . . .
Judge not: whatever floats your Prologue boat!
    So drowning in his grief, DJ bought, well,
a Mae West – which I think is only fair,
for what is poetry but fashioned air?

Our DJ sought a love-life off the rack,
    so bought a blow-up doll one afternoon
from 'Guys & Dolls', whose owner loves the crack
    and said he'd 'Muslim Dolls' arriving soon –
'they blow themselves up!' DJ volleyed back:
    *'And what's the difference between a balloon
and a squaddie? A balloon doesn't scream
when it's . . .'* Enough! Sad men letting off steam

do not behave in ways you'd call PC –
    foreshortened wisdom of the acronym!
To some, DJ and I show ADD,
    so telescoping all of me and him
in fashionable terminology:
    We're men of letters, yet you're just as dim
about the way our characters were set.
Does poetry transcend its alphabet?

Now DJ's blow-up doll he called Camilla,
    lending his intent a certain thrill;
it might not be a cooer or a biller –
    but neither did it baulk at DJ's will;
in looks, his doll more truly was a killer
    than she whose place it was designed to fill,
a Cicciolina to our hero's Koons.
The real Camilla hates how DJ moons

about – she loved another kind of bore
    whose fire was cool and mathematical,
(you might think here she's settling some old score . . .)
    while DJ's passion was fanatical.
Camilla'd met such drama kings before –
    emotionally autocratical,
hollow inside yet still narcissistic –
she only liked real shells to go ballistic.

But his doll stayed when standards were unfurled,
    unstirred to hear some distant bugle's sound,
pneumatic as that girl in *Brave New World*:
    ideal for DJ's desperate rebound.
Back home, he dived right on – to be then hurled
    arse over tit and dick-first to the ground,
where he lay groaning like a poet when
he bends beyond repair his favourite pen.

Desire to be a poet once seemed mad,
    yet nowadays such itches seem much madder;
insanity in poets might seem sad,
    but sanity among them's even sadder;
the times for poetry are worse than bad,
    with baby boomers pulling up the ladder,
jackal poets fighting for what's left.
By class again the UK is now cleft

in ways once thought consigned to history,
  reflected in contemporary taste
between its various kinds of poetry;
  some jewels in England's crown are so much paste
while naked emperors are quick to see
  the land around their ivory towers as waste.
If Byron sniffed a bit at rhyming cobblers,
the lords of verse today are throwing wobblers.

Lord Ashdown likened Clegg to Lochinvar,
  the misty-eyed old soldier that he is,
which I thought rather stretching things too far:
  the chivalry he senses is just his;
behind the lines is where Nick Clegg's a wiz
  at bayoneting wounded in a war:
dispatching Gordon Brown, none could be slicker:
Clegg could claim his motto's, '*I Mak Siccar*'.

Some foe was dubbed 'MacSikker' by Geoff Hill,
  among we dwarfish poets a Magog;
this heavyweight contender tops the bill
  with Jerry Prynne, his alter ego Gog.
The outcome of their contest's undecided still,
  being fought in an impenetrable fog –
is Prynne why now your average college nerdsworth
shuns Byron to study bloody Wordsworth?

But we must go: the whip's cracked by Apollo,
  champing, like his horses, at the bit.
From him this 'god of verse' guff's rather hollow,
  given his unsubtle view of it,
but he's my god and his line I must follow –
  reader: I can't serve you as is fit;
he won't accept digression has a function,
never mind ellipsis or disjunction.

So: we're back upon the straight and narrow,
  like DJ's road to agonizing hell
where now he'll nurse his blunted Cupid's arrow,
  proudest when upon it DJ fell . . .
What happens to him now? Consult the tarot.
  Our time's up: Apollo rings the bell
for one whose bell-end here's been wrung so hard;
who'll live, though hoisted with his own petard,

unlike another as a new day broke:
  the real Camilla finds an IED . . .
no scream (as in sad DJ's bitter joke),
  a shivering of air is all you see,
a mirage mirroring a puff of smoke.
  The letter killeth still, believe you me –
of course you can't. Her death's another lie.
In worlds of letters, only authors die.

Mother Shipton

I know you'll pass the World's End bar
to cross that river by the well
whose water changes time to stone
to find our Yorkshire Sibyl's home.

You'll know her face's sickle moon
from moth's wings, Punch, old bills for plays,
her metred words of metered fate
from Pepys, Defoe, the internet.

In her unending ending worlds,
hares make our hearths their birthing beds,
a thorn hangs horses, swords plough fields
while one-eyed women wade through blood.

What all this means, the wise don't ask,
but watch from shadows in her cave
dead metaphors escape their grave
to breathe again behind her mask.

Ashtrayville

Imagine a city. It is not a city you know,
although it seems familiar as you walk
towards it down a road full of pot-holes
under an arcade of colourless rainbows.

You might try to negotiate the pot-holes
but they are not open to negotiation –
the road only says, take it or leave it.
You turn yet find yourself inside the city.

In deserted avenues of birdless trees,
the houses are implausibly magnificent,
like the ghosts of old-fashioned lunatics
in costumes of *ancien régime* fantasies.

All the paving stones have been stolen,
so you walk down the centre of streets
till one chooses you, its second choice,
you realize, one untaken before now.

Tar glints as if with watchmakers' quartz,
as if you have appointments and are late.
You walk faster, your feet fitting perfectly
the footprints in the ash as thick as snow.

You meet a man wearing black overalls.
He says he's painting double yellow lines,
but the road has never seen any traffic.
You notice the paint in his pot is black.

His shadow paints itself into the corner
of your eye, your blind spot. He winks.
His glass eye glints like the quartz heart
of the silent watch he presents you with.

The watch is inscribed in copperplate
with your name, your title, your dates,
that it's for your long service to this city.
You weep with pride. Then you just weep.

The Passion of the Holly

(air: 'The Sans Day Carol')

We're the Sans Day carolers who call once a year;
if we're sans bread and sans brass, we are not sans care,
for the coming of Jesus, born poor to be king
and the passion of the holly at Christmas we sing.

O the holly bore a berry as white as a bone,
for we sing of one new life but many more gone,
so we sing for those grieving as all theirs who died,
whether Christian or not at this cold Christmastide.

But the holly bore a berry as green as new grass,
as Our Lady bore Jesus who died on the cross,
and if summer seems laid in the sepulchre's night –
no dark hold's so strong it's not broken by light.

When the holly bore a berry as black as a mine,
we lit thirty-three candles like Christ's years, a sign;
for poor miners give daylight their living to make,
and some sacrificed more when the holly wore black.

Now the holly bears a berry as Christ's blood it's red,
for the Christ-child means good that can rise from the dead;
and much sharper than holly was Jesus's crown,
and yet he was raised up and Lord Satan cast down.

O our holly and its berry were soon turned to dust,
as were we who in singing and kindness put trust;
and yet though we sing now to you from the grave,
you can hear us because we are singing of love.

Long Will

Langland's my name   long gone from this land
where lettered and lout   alike my tongue lashed;
I'd flay fellow-clerics   for failing their flocks
as fast as the riff-raff   for riot and wrath,
as fiercely as princes   who prey on the poor –
wealth is mere theft   wed into or won,
inherited wealth   as heinous a haul.
My poem gave watchwords   to Wat's men and women
who rose in rebellion   against England's wrongs.
Now I'm brought back   by a fart of a bard,
to rage and to rant   in my *rum, ram, ruff* staves –
a rough and rude roar   in my own raw age,
a savage sound now   upon this sod's soft ears.
I'll make his ears smart   your sorryarse sinner,
a smug poetaster,   posturing pen-pusher
who'd write off religion   as simply a relic
of spent superstitions   from centuries past.
He'd sneer at the prayers   of penitent paupers
whose hope in His heaven   is all hope they have;
he'll tell you that medicine   mends all ill men –
what pills or potions   preserve poisoned souls?
Paul's letters that kill   are the kind of this clerk,
vanity's vessel,   void of all spirit.
Where I look with longing   for lines true and straight,
the pen cutting plain   as Piers' ploughshare
unveeringly drawn   from verse-end to verse-end,
I find instead fiddling   as fancy as Frenchmen's

or rhyme chancer Chaucer   chose for his poesy;
where I look for rhythms   rum, rough and ramming,
wholesome and heavy   as plough-horse's hooves,
I'm bored stiff by beatless,   babyish rattlings,
unmeasured metre   men's feet can't march to;
no clashing of consonants   but cowardly vowels
softening such combat   to simpering songs.
His maundering minstrelsy's   destined for mulch,
pulp spread like gullshit   in Piers Ploughman's wake,
feeding His fields   for heavenly bread
whose hymns and hosannas   will rise sweet and high
when people will praise   without poets' help
the grandeur and glory   of God and His works.

In His Shadow

I would say that knowing is a road.
— Anne Carson

Colourful Blind Jack would see right through me,
colourless beside all his many coats and trades,
technicolour escapades my dull ink must betray.

A Froggie-lover like those he saw off at Culloden,
he'd scorn me stumbling *commes sur les pavés*,
how I used that line from Baudelaire for a crutch,

my fiddle with words while his own played tunes
Jack had only to hear once to know backwards.
He played to lead the Yorkshire Blues into battle.

Women fell for him too, even later on in his life
when Jack always stunk of pitch like Old Nick.
He could sweet talk alright, to get somewhere.

Testing stones to bed his roads' black tongues,
I heard how Jack rolled them around his mouth
'like new words'. But I wouldn't know about that.

Opening Night

Sartre turned white-faced with excitement when a colleague arrived hotfoot from Germany with the news that one could make philosophy out of the ashtray.
— Terry Eagleton, *Guardian*, 12/11/14

The artist, this night's star,
recast a plastic ashtray
and stamped it ASTRAY
for Hamilton's *Ricard*
and *astra*'s Greek roots.

We moon about her art.
Tam leans back to say,
a Glaswegian Sartre,
Life's jis' an ashtray:
a' fu' o' wee doots.

Sardana

Named from *tàpia*, Catalan for wall, his picture
Sardana takes the floor, pediscript of the dance
Franco banned, feet silent as poetry's on a page.
I wait on for an *Introit*, a wallflower in a trance.

The Buddha's aniconic icon once was footprints:
Tàpies followed them to Shaolin's Bodhidharma,
who gazed silently for nine years on his cell wall
to bore a hole shaped like the wheel of samsāra.

After silence, my paintings became their walls,
he wrote; they opened like Alice's looking-glass
onto galaxies of wonderlands like clouds of dust
rising in town squares as sardana dancers pass.

The Rûm District

It was there for the taking:
the Emperor's soldiery drunken; its golden birds
flown; mosaics dropping from walls;
iconoclastic barbarians at the gate
already calling this world *Rûm*.

Rûm gave its name to Romania.
Romanian wannabe, I holiday at Bucharest's
Grand Hotel Abyss but find myself
watching television – that very word
a cocktail of Greek and Latin, like Rûm.

But the Hotel set's picture seems made
of tesserae rather than pixels,
and its only channel National Geographic
commending whatever is begotten,
born and torn to pieces.

I plunder the minibar, then under the influence
of Xavier de Maistre
embark on a little room travel of my own,
sailing the New Jerusalem of my rented cube
from Revelation through the night of Rûm.

I dream of the poet Rûm calls Rumi,
who tells me the Arabic word for house
names an Arabic poem's unit,
then I wake up in this stanza,
my head spinning like a dervish.

Stanza meaning room, I ring room service
for the hair of the dog, ordering this
rûm cocktail which arrives with an orange slice,
an ash berry, and an ice cube
melting like this poem.

Riddle

Who I am's child's play,
a cry in a kindergarten;
though I pun on Latin,
my Yorkshire kin's *laik*,

a whole lexical rainbow
unweaving in no code,
no masonic *Mahabone*
nor Horseman's Word –

but I'm caltrops at night
to the bare feet of adults
inspiring their language
to such colours as I am,

Kulla, Mondrian plastic
pixellating Mies blocks;
the Ephesian Artemis
in each cubist bust;

the Song of Amergin
by a Turing machine:
name me or you'll be
thicker than any brick.

Brick Arch

If you think of Brick, you say to Brick, 'What do you want, Brick?'
And Brick says to you, 'I like an Arch.'

— Louis Kahn

Cradling a ceramic-finished Glöck
in Iraq where Jesus will fight Dajjal
our clay grown tall patrols his base,
watching children mould clay birds
as Jesus did in St Thomas' Gospel,
before He killed the informer children.

*

With china worth more than gold,
the Saxon court alchemist is set
to turn out at first dinner services,
finally a life-sized Saxon soldiery.
Dresden shivers in the bomb sights
of Prussian artillery, Allied bombers.

*

Qin Shih Huangdi's clayworkers
wound serpent upon clay serpent
till they rose to serve as soldiers
he would later toast in quicksilver,
his court alchemists' prescription
for an emperor who'd live for ever.

[44]

*

Baked clay tablets from Babylon tell
how bricks had symbolized creativity,
with The Mother of Us All, Belet-ili,
praised as 'Our Brick of Lapis Lazuli';
how bricks from then to now dimple
as if impressed by her curving belly.

Give Me Your Hand

*After Daedalus' first song in Jonson's
'Pleasure Reconciled to Virtue'*

You go, I come: I come, you go;
we interweave our angry knot.
I would be friend: you think me foe
or something worse, I don't know what.

Like hares, we spar then dodge away,
pull back, push forward, never stay —
don't let our dancing steps contend:
you lead, I'll follow; be my friend.

We've two left feet, but of one mind
our stumbling could still trace a dance
that harmonizes laws of chance
with laws of art and being kind.

Feet make all roads, Machado says;
just walking makes all walkers' ways
as only dancing keeps the maze
from hungry grass in Shakespeare plays.

Confucius, who'd make rulers wise,
admired the wisdom of the feet
where, without force, we keep our beat,
and made dance stately exercise.

Philosophers like Collingwood
saw dance as more than social good
and how its turning feet could be
the pattern of all poetry.

So take my hand now, take the time;
roll past and future in a ball
till here and now our bodies rhyme.
For soon we won't, for good and all.

Square Ring

for Tom Duhig

A Sixties man thing: Dad, us, circling to bond
as hard as Ingemar Johansson's glue in the ad
around our huge box, its screen a snow globe
of American static. The night Johansson won,
a commentator summarized Floyd Patterson:
the feet of a ballet dancer, the chin of a poet.
Floyd knocked out Ingemar in their rematch;
his brilliant smile shone through his glass jaw.

Later, I learned how outside ring lights boxing
was darkened by money. Abroad, Henry Cooper
said you needed to knock out locals for a draw.
Some Yanks dived so as not to swim in concrete
boxing boots. My poet's foot is in my mouth now,
Tom, Middleweight Champion of the Royal Navy,
but I remember Freddie Mills staring down a rifle
in the back of that car on his soul's darkest night.

You might counter with Dick 'Tiger', born Ihetu,
burning bright despite suffering the 'blacklights',
those galaxies only battered fighters can explore.
Generous, Dick gave away age, weight or height
but never heart, slipping cannibal taunts to win;
Biafran civil warrior later, yet a hero to both sides –
another trick of boxing: it can also make more love.
Square that ring, poet! Brother, raise your hands.

Contracted Silences

1

Antonio Stradivari stalks the Forest of Violins,
kicking trees for close-ringed echoes made
later by his Messiah, now the Ashmolean's,
bequeathed on condition it be never played.

2

Debbie Reynolds,
ghost singer Kathy
in *Singin' in the Rain*
had a ghost singer
as unsung again.

In *Debbie: My Life*,
Reynolds names her,
only to spell it wrong.
I right it here: *Noyes*.
This noise is her song.

3

A sean-nós singer I heard in Larne one day,
being a Protestant from the Glens of Antrim,
suffered for his tadhg art threats of violence

till at last he got the message from the UDA:
give it a rest or there's a contract out on him.
After that, as the man said, the rest is silence.

The White Page

Poets don't draw. They unravel their handwriting
and then tie it up again, but differently.
— Jean Cocteau

If you stretch out this writing
into one long, thin single line,
draw it to an invisible thread,

you can make its information
your own material, giving you
the whip-hand over this verse,

this universe – then with a flick
of your wrist, it will ripple into
a silhouette of your own fancy,

a portrait of Widow Wadman
left blank in *Tristram Shandy*
by Sterne for your realisation

in Cixous' ink, or like letters
Molly Bloom sends herself
with love's blind signature.

Bridled Vows

I will be faithful to you, I do vow,
but not until the seas have all run dry
et cetera. Although I mean it now
I'm not a prophet and I will not lie.

To be your perfect wife, I could not swear;
I'll love, yes; honour (maybe); won't obey,
but will co-operate if you will care
as much as you are seeming to today.

I'll do my best to be your better half,
but I don't have the patience of a saint
and at you, not with you, I'll sometimes laugh,
and snap too, though I'll try to show restraint.

We might work out. No blame if we do not.
With all my heart, I think it's worth a shot.

The Full Weight of the Law

i.m. Manuel Bravo

Let me be weighed in an even balance. But I was not:
The scales fell from my eyes while Justice stayed blind,
her scale pans pennies lifted from a dead man's eyes.
My lawyer didn't show and I was mute at my tribunal.

When I came to this land of [uz] I learned its languages,
its poetry, Shakespeare, King James' Bible, its weather:
By the breath of God frost is given, He saith to the snow,
Be thou on the earth; likewise to the small rain. In time,

I even got to like it: *Hast thou entered into the treasures*
of the snow? Or hast thou seen the treasures of the hail?
Hail like uncut diamonds from my home, blood diamonds.
More than it siling, I liked rain merciful, that droppeth slow.

I found out I had lost but that my son Antonio could stay
if I should die. So my immortal soul was a small forfeit,
as light as that feather of truth in those scales of Anubis
we saw on a papyrus scroll on our visit to Leeds Museum.

God stretcheth out the north over the empty place and
hangeth the earth upon nothing. With its twisted sheets,
I weigh myself in Yarl's Wood detention centre stairwell,
my soul chooseth strangling, and death rather than life.

The Scripture of the Jade Pivot

When he began to study *The Scripture of the Jade Pivot*,
the prince my husband's disposition changed, he became
terrified whenever he saw the characters for 'jade' or 'pivot',
and of the jade pivot charms given to him at the May festival
to ward off disasters. Also from this time on he grew terrified
of the sky, and the characters for 'thunder' and 'thunderclap'.
He murdered the eunuch Kim Han-ch'ae, bringing his head
impaled on a stick to frighten the ladies of his father's court.

When the king summoned his son to Sùngmun-dang Hall
for questioning over this and similar incidents, the prince
replied, 'It relieves my pent-up anger, Sire, to kill people
or animals when I'm depressed.' The king asked him why,
and the prince replied, 'Because I am hurt by you, father,
because you do not seem to love me.' Then he confessed
to the exact number of those he'd killed: many court maids,
a blind fortune-teller, several translators and physicians.

When the prince asked me to come to him the next day,
a great cawing flock of magpies rose up, surrounding
Kyongch'un-jon Mansion. 'What an omen!' I thought.
Arriving then at the Toksong-hap Audience Chamber,
I feared he would fly into new a rage at the sight of me,
but he just said, 'I have a sense that they will let you live.'
Then, astonishingly, he suggested we run away together.
We both wept on hearing the horses in the courtyard.

At four o'clock in the afternoon of the appointed day
when the king ordered that his son be interred alive,
it rained heavily and the thunder rolled across the sky.
The grain box was buried underneath his palace lawn.
This was proper, something I would not dare to criticize.
I was spared to be responsible for the royal grandson.
My gratitude is so deep that it is engraved on my bones.

Aliens

Simon Parkes, Labour councillor for the Stakesby ward of Whitby,
claimed at a public meeting recently that Russia's President Putin
is being advised by warlike aliens Councillor Parkes calls 'Nordics'.

He went on to describe how his own father was, in fact, a 'Nordic',
how he himself had lost his virginity to a female of this alien species
and continues to have regular sexual intercourse with her to this day.

All this might seem unlikely to a stranger – even the name Stakesby,
for example, could suggest an allusion to Whitby's vampire heritage,
as 'Nordics' to other aliens invading these shores a millennium ago.

Yet I too have seen on this coast the most astonishing phenomena,
the aurora borealis dancing like the hem of a Byzantine silk dress,
inexplicable diamond lights at sea, flying creatures I cannot name.

Once I saw a woman of matchless beauty walking along this shore,
her dress a liquefaction of the Northern Lights, unutterable colours.
Her hair rolled in golden waves. Her eyes glinted like splintered jet.

For a second, they held my gaze; blood-red lips parted; I glimpsed
a reef of teeth as white as the breaking surf. However fast I walked,
I could not catch up with her. Fearing to look importunate, I fell back.

And she was already gone, her dress a glimmer of oil in a rock pool
like the cloak sea-women leave in stories. How long ago was all this?
More than forty years. I come back often. I never stop looking for her.

Selkie

sea land sky seal
sees land seal lands
on sand selkie stands
high wide-eyed slim spry
shiny skin shivers slides
melts to man flesh light
fins split to fingers feet
idles a time decides
turns to try inland
his lively lady luck
fly finds a shoal
lassies laughing flashing
teeth knives slit fish slice
cran creel reel selkie sings
singles out one silver darling
shawl white shoulders slipping
sidles alongside selkie smiles
gives glad eye feeds lines
lies easily so soft words
aye ye o why why not
lie beside me o my lady
list while I lilt a lay lady
a lullaby a lull my lovely
say aye o she says so
o selkie kisses sea smell
he slips inside her slight slip
unstays her white stays o so

she melts as salt in water says
o o fish mouths o yesyesyesyes
sweet sin sip sap lick lap slip slap
selkie swells sea swell tide roll break o
she shivers pleasured flesh ocean rush
hush my love shshshshshshshshshshsh
she's a shell sea shell shhhhh
he eases she pleased sleeps
he seems asleep lies still sly
by and by says bye bye
silently smiles slips away
quick stops on slipway
see seal skin again
melt wave sea waves
turns inland seal waves
webbed hand flash fin

ACKNOWLEDGEMENTS AND NOTES

A number of these poems, or some very like them, have already appeared elsewhere. Thanks are therefore due to the editors of *Poetry Review*, *Poetry* (US), *The Poetry Review*, *The Edinburgh Review*, *Canto*, *Compose*, *Poetry & Audience*, *The Lifeboat* (Belfast), *The Dark Horse*, the *Guardian*, *Poetry London*, *Poetry Salzburg Review*, *The Moth*, *Thirteen Pages*, *Contourlines: New Responses to Landscape in Word and Image* (ed. Neil Wenborn and M.E.J. Hughes, Salt 2009), *In Their Own Words* (ed. George Szirtes and Helen Ivory, Salt 2012), *A Modern Don Juan* (ed. Andy Croft & N.S. Thompson, Five Leaves Publications 2014), *Versions of the North: Contemporary Yorkshire Poetry* (ed. Ian Parks Five Leaves Publications 2013), *Digressions* (with Philippa Troutman, Smokestack 2014), *Interventions* (Poetry School CAMPUS Pamphlet 2015).

'The Marbled Page' was written for a Shandy Hall fundraising project called 'The Emblem of My Work' and appeared in the Laurence Sterne Trust exhibition and 2013 catalogue of that name.

'Half the Story' relates to a story recorded by Dora Diamant, but I came across it first from Anthony Rudolf, whose 'Kafka and the Doll' is recommended.

'Indirections' refers to the City of Troy turf maze not far from Shandy Hall, where according to tradition you can lose the Devil as he can only move in straight lines. This and other poems here originally formed part of 'Digressions', a site-specific project for the tercentenary of Sterne's birth involving art by Philippa Troutman, poetry and prose with some shape-shifting between the last two written by the present author. Its launch and first art exhibition took place at the Poetry Society in the Autumn of 2014, for which we gratefully acknowledge the support of Judith Palmer and Mike Sims especially among the staff there, as ACE which funded the project. The 'Afterforeword' from the *Digressions* book describing the project's procedures and background are viewable at philippatroutman.com

In 'Shapeshifting Ghosts of Byland Abbey', the background details concerning the monk's manuscript, and James' comments in his published selection of them in Latin, are accurate, although when I visited Byland Abbey its staff professed no knowledge of this text, the original monastic manuscript or the ghost stories described therein.

'The White Page' alludes to Simon Morris's project 'Information as Material' (iam), often involved with Shandy Hall, now a recognized international centre for conceptual writing.

'The Blue Queen of Ashtrayland' quotes Skeeter's song from Bernard Hare's account of a particularly marginalized Leeds gang of school and social dropouts, *Urban Grimshaw and the Shed Crew* (Sceptre 2006), 'Ashtrayland' being Urban's name for an England whose history, politics and culture are remote from and irrelevant to the Shed Crew's lives, a mirror-image of the views expressed by Conservative MP Mark Garnier, who in 2014 referred to 'dog-end voters' living in 'the outlying regions of Britain' with whom his party need not concern itself.

'Sternomancy': 'An Irish bull' is related to the expression 'a cock and bull story'. As in *Digressions*, the names of

[60]

Asterion and Sterne are more than cognate and 'stern(e)' is also a Scots word for star.

'The Balladeer's Lament': A form is a hare's nest.

'Canto': Byron described Don Juan as 'a poetical *Tristram Shandy'*. Commissioned as an updating of Byron's poem, I have attempted to give the speaker of mine views in keeping with the frequently outrageous spirit of the original.

'Ashtrayville': The first line is taken from Anthony Thwaite's poem 'Imagine a City'.

'Becky Beasley's *Astray* is a brass cast of a cheap plastic hotel ashtray with the word "Astray" added in Gloucester MT Extra Condensed lettering. Technically a malapropism, the omission of the letter "h" from the word ashtray (a nod to Richard Hamilton's iconic addition of the letter "h" to the French Ricard ashtray to write Richard) opens up a wild new dimension to the work, whilst also highlighting the Greek root word, Astra, meaning from the stars.' (Exhibition catalogue, South London Gallery, October 2014)

'Sardana': The introit is the opening phase of this traditional Catalonian dance.

'The Rûm District' is based on Sam Gwynn's Ashbery squib, 'The Rum District'.

'The Full Weight of the Law' makes reference to the case of Manuel Bravo, a Leeds asylum seeker from Angola, who fled to the UK after his pro-democracy activity led to attacks on his family, including the murder of his parents. At Manuel's asylum hearing, his solicitor did not attend and he was forced to represent himself, without understanding the nature of the legal proceedings in which he was engaged. He did not learn that his claim for asylum had been finally refused until his removal to Yarl's Wood Immigration Removal Centre. His son Antonio was allowed to remain in this country.

'The Scripture of the Jade Pivot': Based on *Memoirs of a Korean Queen* by Lady Hong, edited and translated by Choe-Wall Yang-hi, in KPI's Korean Culture Series 1987.

'Aliens' and 'Selkie' formed part of the site-specific project 'Interventions', which was commissioned by Dorcas Taylor of Wordquake and funded by the Poetry School, who published the subsequent pamphlet. The installation of these and a number of concrete poems in the house and grounds of Sewerby Hall and their exhibition took place over the summer of 2015.